S0-AHB-853

Ruth Joyce Yanish's Memoirs
Stories of the Joyce Family
1926-1950

Ruth Joyce Yanish

© 2012 Ruth Joyce Yanish
All Rights Reserved.

No part of this publication may be reproduced, stored in a retrieval system, or transmitted, in any form or by any means, electronic, mechanical, photocopying, recording, or otherwise, without the written permission of the author.

First published by Dog Ear Publishing
4010 W. 86th Street, Ste H
Indianapolis, IN 46268
www.dogearpublishing.net

ISBN: 978-145751-188-2

This book is printed on acid-free paper.

Printed in the United States of America

To forget one's ancestors is to be a brook without a source, a tree without a root.

(A Chinese Proverb)

Pictures

Ma and Pa in their wedding photo - 1912

Ann and John Joyce

ANN DUGAN WAS A LOVELY Irish lass living on a farm in Tuam, Ireland. She was born in June. Her sisters, Mary and Kate, had immigrated to Boston early in the turn of the twentieth century and encouraged Ann to join them. So she sailed alone from Ireland to the Port of Boston in 1911. In Boston, she found a job as a domestic housekeeper in Milton, Massachusetts. She did that for a while until her friend, Margaret Wheeler, told her that the Harvard Knitting Mills in Wakefield, where Margaret worked, was hiring. Ann applied for the job and was hired. She was able to stay at the same boarding house on Albion Street with her friend and other girls who also worked at Harvard Knitting Mills. Ann had been lonesome, working as a housekeeper, but now she had lots of friends. On Sundays, they'd walk around Wakefield's common. This was a beautiful green area near Lake Quanapowitt. It had inviting benches scattered around. While the young Irish girls were enjoying the common, a group of young Irish lads were walking in the same area. Among them was John Joyce, a tall, handsome blue-eyed young man.

John was born in June, had emigrated from county Mayo in 1911 and arrived at the Port of Boston, and now lived at the Crescent House on Water Street in Wakefield. He worked at the Heywood Wakefield Furniture Factory.

Eventually, Ann and John met, fell in love and married in October 1913. Bill was born a year later (October 28, 1914) then Mary (March 28, 1916), Kay (May 1, 1918), Dot (November 14, 1919) and Ruth (October 6, 1921). Ruth had a twin sister, Claire who died sadly at only two months of age. She's buried in a cemetery in Stoneham Massachusetts. These stories are about this family of seven.

Ma and Pa

MA (ANN) AND PA (JOHN) were hard-working, thrifty, and devoted to their family. Ma washed and ironed clothes every day. She cooked a big dinner every night. At that time, there were few packaged goods, so it took a long time to prepare a big dinner. If we said we liked her stew, she'd make it again and again. She wanted us to enjoy our meals.

Pa worked at the Heywood Wakefield Furniture Factory and later for the town. He worked hard at any job he could get to earn money for his family. He was a substitute policeman every Halloween guarding the red fireboxes around town. He also collected brass to sell to Mr. Levine, the junkman.

Ma was quiet and shy, but Pa was outgoing. He liked to talk and listen to everyone. Pa was kind-hearted and ready to help his friends. If a friend wanted a beer, Pa would give it to him. Ma didn't always like that, but Pa would explain that the man needed a drink and, as importantly, a friend. Once he had a friend visiting who was a barber. He stayed a long time. Pa and the barber started drinking. Then Pa had a great idea. He asked the barber to give everyone a haircut. We all got haircuts, although the barber was quite tipsy by then. I wonder what we looked like when the job was finished?

Ma never yelled and scolded, but we knew how she wanted us to behave, and tried not to disappoint her.

Ma and Pa had many friends in the neighborhood, who'd gather at our house to play Whist, their favorite card game. After the game, Ma would serve tea and cookies. Most of the time, our household was happy and peaceful.

Not just a name upon a tree, the Lord has made us family, to share our lives both good and bad. To come together, happy or sad.

The Crescent House

THE CRESCENT HOUSE WAS AN imposing gray house on Water Street in Wakefield. It had a spacious front porch with several rocking chairs scattered around. The Crescent House served as a boarding house for young bachelors, many of whom worked at the nearby Heywood Wakefield Furniture Factory. Pa was one of those young men. He had emigrated from County Mayo, Ireland for a better life in America, and found work at the furniture factory.

Pa enjoyed his stay at the Crescent House. He often told his daughters of his exploits while living there, of the interesting men who lived with him, and of the great meals served. The story we heard most often, concerned the efficient manner of their kitchen cleanup. According to Pa, 15 minutes after dinner was over the ladies had cleaned the kitchen proficiently and were in their rocking chairs, resting. Pa's four daughters strived to imitate the Crescent House ladies, but their cleanup lasted about an hour, accompanied by loud voices and pot banging.

Pa loved his daughters and celebrated their talents. However, he was disappointed that their skills did not include efficient kitchen cleanup. We never did attain the standards of the Crescent House ladies.

Pa and Mary and Dot

Pa's Favorite Things

- Pa's Favorite Game for Children: Pa would sit on a chair, and one of us would lie across his lap, face down. Then, alternating between his hands and elbows he's recite this ditty: Hurley- burley, trump the key, the cow jumped over the garden wall, Simon Alley, hunt the buck, how many fingers stand up? We'd guess how many fingers; no prizes were ever awarded.
- Pa's Favorite Expression: She can talk the legs off a stool.
- Pa's Financial Advice: When you get a pay check, put some of the money in the bank immediately, before you spend any.
- Pa's Health Advice: Get fresh air, sunshine and exercise every day.
- Pa's Social advice: Be friendly to all.
- Pa's Favorite Foods: Boiled potatoes and soft boiled eggs (in an egg cup).

The greatest gift came from afar, it came from God, and I call him Pa

Ma, Pa, Ruth and the Keefe Kids

Ma's Favorite Things

- Favorite Singer: Bing Crosby.
- Favorite Sport: Sitting in the shade, never in the sun.
- Favorite Time of Day: Evenings, reading the Wakefield Item newspaper to Pa, and discussing local events.
- Health Advice: Eat wholesome foods.
- Social Advice: be a good Catholic.

A precious gift from heaven above is the gift of a mother for a daughter to love
Some of Ma's Favorite Dishes

- Gingerbread served hot with real whipped cream.
- Fish Stew – white fish, onions, potatoes, butter and milk.
- Cod fish cakes.
- Corn chowder with corn, onions, potatoes, butter, milk, sometimes bacon, but not on Friday.
- Turnover – made from leftover pie crust. Roll out a square of crust. In middle of crust add sugar and cinnamon. Fold over four ways and bake until brown.
- Mashed potatoes with lots of butter and cream. Make sure you crush the potatoes with a potato masher.

Brother Bill

BILL WAS ALWAYS GOOD-NATURED AND hard working. Pa spent a lot of time repairing things around the house, and would usually enlist Bill's help. Pa would say "Hold this – it will only take a minute". In reality, it would often take 40 minutes. If Bill was not home, Pa would grab whatever girl was closest.

I was Bill's youngest sister so he was always asking me to do things for him. He said once: "That's why God gave me a young sister". I'd shine his shoes, find his hat, and run errands for him. I did everything he asked willingly, as sometimes I'd get a dime. In those days, I'd do anything for a dime.

By high school age, Bill was a very good looking fellow. He had dark hair, blue eyes, and straight white teeth. Often, the girls in the neighborhood would be friendly to me. I didn't know why, until they'd start talking about Bill. They wanted an introduction to him. I'd do my best, but Bill usually wasn't interested. He wanted to choose his own girlfriends.

I've been blessed to have a brother like you; you're my pal, my buddy, my best friend too. One thing I'd like to suggest; that of all the brothers in the world, you're the best

Mary

Sister Mary

MARY WAS THE OLDEST GIRL and was often like a little Mother to Kay, Dot and me, which we didn't always like. We'd go into the living room to relax for a few minutes after dinner. Inevitably, Mary would say cheerfully "Let's all go clean up the kitchen." We'd go because we knew she'd persist.

Mary was mature and responsible. She worked at the Public Works Department in Boston when she was 19. She was in Boston where the best buys were, so Ma and Pa trusted her to select small appliances for the family. She even bought us a refrigerator once. Ma and Pa would never allow us other girls to buy expensive articles.

Mary was a hard worker, and would gladly help Ma clean house. The others three girls would help, although a bit reluctantly.

Mary was generous. She'd often bring us a treat from Boston, such as candy or dessert.

Ma and Pa were lucky that their oldest girl was such a help to them. Thankfully, they never compared Kay, Dot, and Ruth to her.

Sisters have a tie that is bound by love

*Ruth, Baby Joe Keefe, Kay and Mary
in Front of 22 Highland Street*

Sister Kay

KAY WAS SMART, ATHLETIC AND funny. She loved all sports and was good at them. She once won a roller skating dance contest. Ma was not impressed as our cousin from Milton won a scholarship to college the same week. Ma hoped Kay would be more academic as she was an honor student in high school. But that didn't interest Kay. She once left her secretarial job to spend the winter skiing in North Conway, New Hampshire. She'd waitress at meal times and ski the rest of the day.

Kay was bolder and more adventurous than Mary, Dot and Ruth. Pa worried about her and was always trying to tame her. Kay had a group of girlfriends in the neighborhood who'd go ice skating, roller skating or dancing. Much to Pa's chagrin, they'd get home very late and say their good-byes loudly, talking and laughing. Pa told Kay many times to get home early and quietly, but she didn't think that was important. She was locked out many times, often spending the night at Jessie Muise's house. One night, when she was locked out, she banged and banged on the door until Pa came downstairs, opened the door, slapped her face, and went back to bed without saying a word. I don't think Pa was able to change Kay, but Kay was always the one who could cheer Pa up and make him feel better by getting him to laugh.

If sisters were flowers, I'd pick you

Bill and Dot

Sister Dorothy (Dot)

DOT AND I WERE CLOSE in age and were good friends when we were growing up. We'd go swimming together and to the playground together. We often had our arms around each other. Do siblings do that now?

When I was in college, Dot was working. She had lots of pretty clothes, much more than I had. She'd leave for work before I did, so I sometimes would borrow a sweater or a blouse. I'd always return it in good condition – and wash it if necessary. Fortunately for me, we were the same size. Dot would scold me for wearing her sweater, but I'd like to think that she was happy that I was such a well-dressed college student.

I can no longer wear her clothes, but she's still my sister and my friend.

The bond of sisters stands the test of time

Ruth

Sister Ruth

RUTH WAS THE YOUNGEST CHILD in the family. She was a shy, quiet girl who loved to read. She was conscientious and hard working. As a result, she did well in school. She had good health during her twelve years of school since she contracted the childhood diseases – chicken pox, measles and mumps from her older sisters and brother before she attended school. As a result, she had perfect attendance in grades one through twelve.

Ruth liked sports and was ready to roller skate, ice skate, ski or swim whenever she could. Although she was not athletic like Kay, her friends didn't mind and would invite her along nevertheless.

When Ruth graduated from Wakefield High School in 1939, the other children were working, so Ma and Pa could afford the $75.00 per year tuition at Salem State Teachers College.

Ruth and Eddie Maloney paid a driver to transport them to college as there was no bus or train service from Wakefield to Salem. The first semester, they rode in a rumble seat. All the students looked cute in their pretty sweaters and jackets. All except Ruth and Eddie. They came to college wearing winter jackets, scarves and hats, looking out of place. That rumble seat was a very chilly place.

After graduating from Salem Teacher College in 1943, Ruth and Margaret Buckley taught school in Peterborough, New Hampshire for one year. Ruth then taught in several towns in Massachusetts, finally teaching first grade at the Franklin School in Wakefield.

Giggles, secrets sometimes tears, sisters and friends throughout the years

Dot, Mary and Katie

Sister-in-Law Katie

BILL'S GIRLFRIEND WAS VISITING US for the weekend. She was pretty, but had a strange New York accent. The first thing Ma offered her was a glass of tonic, which to a New Yorker meant medicine, but to a Bostonian meant soda. Bill explained it to Ma. Ma and Katie liked each other immediately. Ma waited on her all weekend, even serving her breakfast in bed. We girls were a little jealous – she never waited on us. Of course, we had no guest room, so Katie had to sleep with Kay. Fortunately, Mary was married and living in Depew, New York.

Eventually Katie and Bill decided to get married. We were all happy except Pa. He was afraid she'd persuade Bill to move to New York. On the weekend of the wedding, we all took the train to the North Station, then the subway to the South Station. Pa stayed home as he didn't yet approve of Bill's choice. As we were waiting for our train, an announcement came over the loudspeaker "Ruth Joyce report to window five. You have a phone call". It was Pa. He had changed his mind, and was coming to Bill's wedding. He wanted to know the name of the hotel where the wedding would take place. I gave him the name of address of the hotel, told him to take a taxi cab from the train station, and bring his best suit. Pa arrived on time. It was a lovely ceremony.

Much to Pa's delight, they settled in Wakefield. Bill was the only one of us in Wakefield, so they were the ones who took care of Ma when she was old. At one time, Ma was in the hospital, in bed for a week. Her legs got so weak, that she could no longer walk. We thought that there was nothing to do but put her in a nursing home. She hated the nursing home. Dot and her boyfriend, Louie, visited her every evening walking her up and down the halls. Eventually, she could walk again. We took her home.

She was happy to be in her own home and choose her own food. Katie and Bill were the ones who took care of her. When they were not available, Katie found caretakers.

Katie took care of her with love and affection, telling her the news of the day, what Bing Crosby, Ma's favorite entertainer, was doing, joking with her, and singing with her. Ma stayed home until a week before she died at 96 years of age. We're all grateful that Katie made Ma's final years, happy ones.

It is a very short trip. While alive, live

Katie and Bill at their wedding

Baby Billy

WHEN KATIE AND BILL HAD their first baby, they lived just three houses away from Ma and Pa. Ma liked that as she's see her darling grandson often. Pa passed Billy's house on his way home from work. If Billy wasn't outside in his carriage, Pa would be annoyed and tell Katie that the baby needs fresh air and sunshine even in cold weather.

Katie began to put Billy out in his carriage just before Pa was due home. That didn't stop Pa's criticism "The baby should be facing the sun"." The baby was too bundled up with blankets". Ma would always say that Katie is a wonderful Mother. She didn't like Pa's criticism, but, of course, he wouldn't stop. I think Katie was glad when they moved to Spaulding Street.

Billy grew up to be a strong healthy baby. Maybe Pa was right about fresh air and sunshine.

Our New House – 1926- the Fire

OUR NEW HOUSE WAS BEAUTIFUL – white with green shutters and a spacious back porch where I knew we'd spend summer evenings, but now it was December. Snow was quietly falling, but we were ready for winter. Last week, Ma took us to the Converse Rubber Factory in Malden for new boots. Mine were black Arctic's with four buckles – beautiful in a useful way. The boots were in the kitchen ready for tomorrow. I went to bed dreaming of sliding down the hill in my brother's Flexible Flyer.

In the dark of night, I woke up to my mother's screaming "The house is on fire. Go out the front door. Don't stop for anything". I stumbled down the stairs, saw flames in the kitchen, and smelled smoke everywhere.

Bill seized a vase of artificial flowers, Mary grabbed her Library book. We hurried to the front door. Our neighbor, Mr. Morgan, was gesturing for us to follow him. We had not met Mr. Morgan, but we would follow anyone to get to shelter.

I was the youngest child, age five and had mumps at the time. Mother, walking barefoot in the snow, carried me. Since we had no telephone, Pa had to rush to the nearest red fire box to pull the lever. We heard the shrill sound of the fire engines and saw the fireman jerking at the hoses. Dot and I were huddled together crying, while Ma tried to comfort us.

The fire was confined to the kitchen, so we returned to our smoky house for the rest of the night. The next day, we saw that the kitchen was destroyed, and that strange smell was of our rubber boots – ruined.

We didn't get any Christmas presents that year, but we did get new boots.

Families give us history, roots tied to our past

Pa, Ruth and Ma

22 Highland Street, Wakefield, Mass.

IN 1926, WE MOVED FROM Melvin Street to Highland Street, Wakefield, Mass. The first thing I noticed about it was that there were many children in the neighborhood.

We all found friends quickly.

The house had a small back yard with an apple tree, and a side yard with a grape arbor. Inside, there were three bedrooms upstairs, one for Ma and Pa, one for Bill and a bigger room for Mary, Kay, Dot and Ruth. We had no privacy. Mary and Kay slept together and Dot and Ruth slept together. In the girl's room we had a four drawer bureau, one drawer each for our clothes and also a small closet. There wasn't much room for clothes, but we had few clothes so it was sufficient.

Downstairs, we had a kitchen, dining room, a living room, and a pantry. In the dining room, Ma had a lovely curved glass china cabinet filled with beautiful dishes, a hot chocolate set, a berry set, a biscuit jar and other attractive dishes.

The kitchen had a big pantry, but no bathroom, just a toilet in the basement. It wasn't easy to take a bath. We had no hot water. We'd heat water on the stove and carry it into the pantry to pour into a basin. If Pa saw one of us taking a bath, he'd encourage another one of us to take one while the water was hot.

Ma had to heat water for the laundry as well. She'd hang the laundry outside on the clothesline even in winter. The clothes would be stiff and still wet when she brought them in to finish drying in the kitchen.

The oak ice chest was in the cellar. Ma would put a card in the window, letting the ice man know how big a piece of ice she wanted. Wearing a rubber apron, the iceman would

lift the ice with huge tongs and haul it down cellar to the ice chest.

Our house was heated by coal and hot air. There was a large register in the dining room. We'd love to stand on it and feel the hot air. The downstairs was warm, but the bedrooms were cold in the winter.

Pa liked our big back porch. He'd sit there and watch the people walk by. There was lots of foot traffic as few people had cars. He'd talk at length to anyone passing by. When they were gone, he'd ask "Who was that?" His eyes were bad, but he loved to talk.

We changed the inside frequently with paint and paper, but not the outside.

My Independence

I HAD MY FIRST TASTE of independence when I was five. Since I was the youngest child in the family, my three older sisters were always taking care of me. One day, my mother said I needed a haircut, and, to my amazement said I could go to the barbershop alone. The barbershop was on Melvin Street where we lived, a short distance away. I felt proud as I walked to the shop with a quarter in one hand and instructions from my mother. "Tell the barber to cut your hair to the middle of your ears. " I liked long hair, but she didn't. The shop was a small white building with rows of jars and bottles with heavenly smells and pretty colors. The barber not only cut my hair, but brushed my neck with powder. Mother greeted me with a smile and a hug "You look good and you smell good".

Our lives are a mosaic of little things

The First Day of School

MA TOOK ME AND MY friend, Emily Sweeney, to the Lincoln School for our very first day of school. I remember the pretty pink velvet hat I wore. We always wore hats in those days.

I had a lovely yellow banana for my recess snack; Emily had a shiny red apple. Miss Poland, the teacher, told us to put our snacks on the windowsills with all the others.

At school, we started the day with a prayer, and a salute to the flag. Soon it was time for recess but my beautiful yellow banana was gone. In its place was Leroy Little's half black banana. Of course, I told the teacher that Leroy had taken my banana. Miss Poland made him give me back my banana and Leroy was angry.

Later, as we all walked home from school, Leroy was behind me and Emily, but he quickly ran ahead, grabbed my hat, spit in it and threw it on the ground. I carried it home, crying and wailing all the way. Ma comforted me and said she could clean it up so it would be as good as new, I learned that day that nobody likes a tattle tale. After that, I tried to solve my problems without involving the teacher.

I heard that Leroy Little grew up to be a fine young man, but to me, he'll always be the boy who spit in my hat.

That it will never come again is what makes life so sweet (Emily Dickinson)

Lincoln School

ALL THE CHILDREN IN THE neighborhood went to the Lincoln School, a big red brick building on a hill. Fortunately it wasn't far as we walked to school and home for lunch.

Mary, Kay and Ruth were good students; Dot and Bill were fair students.

There were not as many rules in school as there are now. The teachers were all women. They would often hit or push the misbehaving boys, never the girls. One boy who was being hit by the teacher said "You can hit me, but first take off those rings".

Along with reading and math, penmanship was an important subject. Raymond Dower, the penmanship teacher, travelled from school to school instructing us in the Zaner Blozer method of hand writing. We'd practice O circles and M lines, often with an eraser on our wrist to assure that we were holding our arms correctly. Mary was left handed but was forced to write with her right hand. She did become a good writer.

Our desks had a hole in the upper right corner for the glass ink well. The teacher would fill it when it was time to write. If a girl had long hair, the boy sitting behind her would be sure to dip her hair in the ink. It was irresistible.

We were patriotic. Every Memorial Day, we'd have an assembly in the large school yard outside our school. Every class had a song to sing. We'd often have a very old Civil War veteran as an honored guest. The Star Spangled Banner was adopted as our national anthem in 1931. Many wanted "My Country Tis of Thee" as the anthem. However, that is the tune of the British National Anthem, so it was rejected.

In the seventh grade, we'd have a bus trip to Salem Willows, an ocean park, ten miles away. We'd swim, enjoy

the rides, eat lunch, and have fun. On the way home, the boys would put starfish down the girl's shirts. Of course, the girls would scream, and jump trying to extract the fish. We always got home safely. Where have all the starfish gone?

Grocery Shopping

EVERY SATURDAY AFTERNOON, MA WOULD do her weekly grocery shopping. She'd choose one of us girls to accompany her. We weren't happy to be chosen as it meant lugging home heavy bags of groceries. Ma would stop first at the A & P store, then at a fruit and vegetable store next door. When she was finished shopping, Ma would have four or five heavy bags to carry the long mile home. Traveling home, we'd stop frequently to rest our tired arms and rearrange the bags which were slowly slipping and sliding to the ground.

If it was icy, the journey was agonizing as Ma had a terrible fear of falling. She would cling tightly to her daughter's arm. Now, the chosen girl would hold Ma up as well as balance the grocery bags. Progress toward home was an inch at a time. We would suggest that Ma take Bill's red wagon, but she always said "no" to that idea. She didn't want to be seen on Main Street pulling a creaky old wagon. As a result, the weekly voyage never changed.

If we ran out of food during the week, Ma would send us to Santoro's Store at the top of Highland Street. We didn't mind that job, unless she needed milk. Milk in glass bottles is very heavy. I wonder if Henry Ford had a similar experience motivating him to build a car!!

Sunday School

EVERY SUNDAY AFTERNOON, WE'D ALL walk to Sunday School, which was held in a building next to the church. Ma gave us 2 cents: one for church and one for candy on the way home. I remember Kay lost one of her pennies on Sunday and quickly said "That's my church penny that I lost" She still had her penny for candy. We'd stop at Lilly's Store on the way home. They had an amazing selection of penny candies –root beer barrels, tootsie rolls, licorice and much more. We spent a long time making a decision, and a long time enjoying it.

One year, Dot won a gold medal for excellence in religion. We were all pleased as very few gold medals were awarded.

I cannot see her but I know she is there. She's my guardian angel, my life with me she shares

Ma and Pa - Dressed for Church

Growing Up Catholic

WE WERE DEVOUT CATHOLICS AND lived by the rules of our religion, the ten commandments. Another rule was to attend Mass every Sunday and the Holy Days of Obligation. We went to confession once a month. I didn't like that rule. We had one Saturday a month for the boys and one Saturday a month for the girls. We'd go on girl's Saturday to the church basement, which was cold in winter and warm in summer. All the catholic girls in town were there, so it was a long wait during which we could do nothing but pray. We then fasted from midnight until we received communion the next day at the 10 o'clock mass, which was the children's mass. There was always someone who fainted, due to the lack of food and the stuffy atmosphere in the church. Every Sunday afternoon, we'd attend Sunday school. We'd study the catechism, which had questions and answers such as "Who made you?" "God made me". "Why did he make you?" "He made me to love him and serve him in this world and the next". We learned it by rote, so we would always remember it.

During Lent, we were expected to fast and sacrifice. We'd usually fast on candy. We'd attend the Stations of the Cross on Fridays.

Our parish had frequent retreats and novenas. I didn't mind going, as we usually went with a group of girls and had fun talking. Sometimes we'd learn something. Many sermons concerned Hell, where we sinners would go. One priest mentioned the dreadful smells in Hell. I had never thought of that type of punishmnent. Now I definitely didn't want to go there.

One time, an older man next to me was making noises. I thought he was groaning at the thought of Hell and damnation, but he was snoring. He apparently was a good-living man with a clear conscience.

We accepted the regulations without question. We joked and laughed often. Our religion did not forbid that.

I am glad I had a religious upbringing. I still pray often and have two favorite saints, St. Anthony and St. Theresa, to whom I pray for intercession. I'll continue to pray for all my friends and relatives.

How will our children know who they are if they don't know where they came from?

Mary's Graduation

JUNE 1933 WAS AN IMPORTANT day for our family. Mary was the first one to graduate from high school. She not only graduated, but she earned the title of Salutarian, the second highest honor in the graduating class. She gave a speech at graduation in front of the entire school, and her proud family. She looked beautiful in a long mint green gown with a marcel wave in her hair. She spoke about Walt Whitman, the poet. Although she practiced at home long and loud, all I can remember is the phrase "I Hear America Singing". Mary graduated at the time of the Great Depression. Nobody, including the school, had extra money. Instead of a scholarship, which schools now give the students, Mary got a year's subscription to the Reader's Digest, a popular monthly magazine.

Mary searched a long time for a job. She finally found a factory job at the Harvard Knitting Mills, a mile and a half from our house. It was a long walk, especially on a cold winter day. She did get frost bitten ears on one cold day.

Eventually, Mary got a civil service job at the Department of Public Works in Boston. It was an easy commute by train. She must have liked it as she stayed a long time.

Children are a poor man's riches

Mary and Bill

Summer Evenings

ON SUMMER EVENINGS AFTER DINNER, none of the boys and girls in the neighborhood were allowed to leave the area. As a result, we all gathered in the small field across the street from our house. There, we played Tag, Hide and Seek, Red Rover, Hoist the Green Sail, and other group games. There would always be arguments and disagreements, but we knew all the games had rules which we couldn't bend or break. I'd ask Bill to let me catch him when we played Tag or Hide and Seek, but he'd always say "No, that wouldn't be fair".

We learned from these games – to share, take turns, compromise, follow the rules, don't whine when you lose, you'll have another turn, don't give up.

Family- another word for love

The Morgan Playhouse

THE MORGAN'S, OUR NEXT DOOR neighbors, had a basement playroom with a wind-up gramophone and lots of records. We'd like to go there on rainy summer days.

Often during the summer, someone would say "Let's put on a show". Then we'd all say "yes, yes!". We could all sing, dance or recite a poem. We'd buy song sheets so we'd know the words to the songs even if the tune was not quite right.

We all thought that we had talent. Nobody told us otherwise.

I remember Kay writing a play about a girl with a hole in her stocking. During the Depression, it was important to keep up appearances. That foolish girl should have darned that hole.

Kay and I had a great song and dance routine for "Tea for Two". We sang "Paper Moon", "Bicycle Built for Two" and other popular songs.

When it was time for the show, we'd invite the parents and any neighborhood children who were not in the show. The charge was one cent which we'd waive if someone didn't have the money. We'd even promise cookies at the end to encourage attendance.

The audience clapped loud and long at the conclusion. We didn't know if we were very good or if they were glad it was over. It did last a long time as we all wanted our time in the limelight.

I wish I could say that some of us got our theatrical start there, but to tell the truth – we started and finished our theatrical careers there.

Lake Quanapowitt

THROUGHOUT OUR CHILDHOOD, WE SPENT many days at Lake Quanapowitt swimming. Ma would make us lunch. We spent the morning swimming and the afternoon at the playground.

The lake had a bathhouse, a small sandy beach, and the beautiful lake. We all learned to swim there. I learned with a pair of water wings. These were made of canvas and rubber with a cloth band between the wings for your body. I'd blow into the wings to inflate them, wear them in the water and feel safe splashing and kicking.

Many times, the Wakefield Item, our local newspaper, would report that the lake was polluted. Then, my friends were not allowed to go swimming, but we Joyce's were. Pa would say "That's ridiculous, it's perfectly safe. You need the exercise, go swimming. Our friends would say "You'll get Typhoid Fever from the water". We went swimming and never got Typhoid Fever. There were always a few other swimmers who didn't think a little pollution would hurt or who didn't read the newspaper.

After eating lunch, we'd go to the playground to ride the swings and see-saws. The playground instructor often had races and contests which we'd enter. We'd get ribbons for winning first place – blue second place- red, third place – yellow. My favorite part of the playground events was the dance program. Dance instructors Ellen and Winnie Ashendon accepted everyone into the program. We practiced all summer, and then put on the program in August to which all the parents were invited.

The one I remember was "The Teddy Bear's Picnic". I loved the dancing and was happy to be a flower dressed in blue and yellow crepe paper.

At the final program, the parents clapped and clapped. We knew we had put on a good show.

That was a good way to spend a summer day.

A heritage that's honored is one that's sure to last

Ma in a dress and Pa in his bathing suit

Nantasket Beach

ONE SATURDAY ON A HOT summer day in the early 1930's, Pa said "Sunday is going to be a sunny day. Who wants to go to Nantasket Beach?" We all squealed with pleasure as we knew a trip to Nantasket meant a boat ride, which sounded like a great adventure to us.

The next day, we walked to the bus which took us to Boston, then boarded another bus to Rowse Wharf. Ma stayed home as she never liked the sun, sand, or water. Pa carried a big bag with our bathing suits and towels.

The boat ride was lively. An accordion player played songs we knew, so we sang along with him. We wandered up and down, and looked out at the other boats. Some of the young people were dancing. All seemed to be having fun. When we left the boat, Pa took us to the Amusement Park which had a merry-go-round, a ferris wheel, and bumper cars. The bumper cars were my favorite. Bill kept bumping me, but I managed to push him into a corner, and ride away. At lunch time, Pa bought us each a hot dog and soda. Then it was time to go to the ocean, our favorite part of the day. We changed in the bathhouse, then rode the waves, walked the beach searching for shells. We made sand castles, and rested on our towels.

It was soon time to get out of our bathing suits and start for home.

The boat ride home was subdued. We didn't feel like getting into the lively mood on the boat. We wanted to sit and rest. The truth was, we were burning with sunburns and then a chill would envelope us.

Pa didn't understand. He was always outside. He was tanned and weather-beaten and had been for years. Pa thought the more sun, the better. When we got home, Ma was sympathetic. She made a bowl of cool tea to put on our

backs with a cloth. According to Ma, the tannic acid in the tea relieved the pain.

I stayed in the house for a week wearing only a cotton slip. I couldn't bear anything else on my sore back.

After that, my girlfriends would invite me to the beach to lie in the sun and get tanned. I'd say "no". I knew my skin didn't like that. One severe sunburn in a lifetime is enough.

What was hard to endure is sweet to recall

The Common in Wakefield, Mass.

LIKE MANY NEW ENGLAND TOWN, Wakefield had a beautiful Common - a green space with benches scattered around. There was also a second common closer to the lake. That's where the playground was located. My sisters and I spent many summer days there, riding the swings, playing the games, and entering contests arranged by the playground instructor. If we won games or contests, we'd get a ribbon, and possibly see our picture in the local newspaper that week.

One summer day, the instructor had a freckle contest. She had only two contestants, both boys. Spotting Kay, she pulled her into the contest; Kay pulled away and sped around the playground with the young instructor sprinting after her. Kay was a fast runner, but as she visualized herself being crowned "Freckle Queen of Wakefield", she was able to double her speed; no one was able to catch her.

A few weeks later, Kay saw an advertisement in a magazine for Peacock cream – guaranteed to fade freckles. It really worked. Kay used it for several weeks until Pa said to Ma: "You have to take Kay to the Doctor – look how pale she is." When Pa heard about the Peacock cream he put a stop to that. A few years later, Kay discovered make-up, which solved her freckle problem. She grew up to be an attractive woman who never left home without applying makeup.

A family stitched together with love seldom unravels

The Boston Skating Rink

KAY LOVED SPORTS OF ALL kinds and she excelled in all of them. She would often take me to the Boston Skating Club. It was a wonderful skating rink used by professional skaters, hockey clubs, and the public. I always looked like a professional as I leaned against the wall. Mary had made a beautiful suit, a black velvet jacket and skirt with a red print lining. Mary often lent it to me. Kay was a good skater; she'd waltz around in the middle of the rink, gracefully turning, skating backwards and on one foot while everyone watched in admiration. I'd cling to the wall, looking, I hoped, like a real skater. Many times, a young man would ask me to skate with him. I'd slip and slide holding him tightly while the young man would politely lead me around, even thanking me for skating with him. I never improved, but I never gave up. I'd be skating still if I only could.

**Other things change but we start and end
with the family**

Ruth in front of The Inn at
North Conway, New Hampshire

Skiing in New Hampshire

ON SNOWY WINTER DAYS IN Wakefield, the neighborhood children would gather on Highland Street to sled and ski. The street was not too steep and not too flat. We approached skiing the same way we approached sledding – get on and enjoy the ride. None of us knew how to stop, turn or other skiing skills. We'd wax the skis, get on the hill and push off. Very often, we'd go downhill at breakneck speed. It's hard to believe that no one ever got hurt. Very few of us had skis. We Joyce's had one pair for the family. We shared them with everyone on the hill.

After World War II, skiing became more popular in America, especially in New Hampshire which had many mountains. The veterans had time and energy for a new sport. The Boston and Maine Railroad had a ski train running on Sundays from Boston's North Station to North Conway. It stopped at several towns including Wakefield. The train left Wakefield at 8:00 a.m., so we'd attend 7:00 a.m. Mass in our ski clothes. The train ride was fun as all the passengers were age 20-29, and did lots of joking and laughing.

North Conway was beautiful with its mountains and evergreen trees. The Austrian ski instructors gave group lessons at the foot of the hill. We'd then practice climbing the hill, stopping on a hill, turning, and other skills. We'd use a rope tow – grab the rope and jump off when we were high enough. There was also a train which we could ride to the top of the mountain. I always came down on the tram as I couldn't ski well enough to ski from the top of the mountain. Wherever we were, we would hear the Austrian instructors call "Bend zee knees."

When we were cold and hungry, we'd go into the huge brown log cabin-like Lodge for hot chocolate, and

hamburgers. We could rest there and watch the skiers through the window.

On the train ride home, there was a photographer who would choose a pretty girl, take her picture, and put it in the next day's newspaper as the Snow Queen of the week.

We all enjoyed our Sundays skiing, but Kay liked it so much that she quit her secretarial job and spent her winter in North Conway waitressing in a restaurant. When she wasn't working, she was skiing. She became an expert, and went skiing as often as she could.

Ruth skiing with her girlfriends

Swamp Skating

WHEN LAKE QUANAPOWITT FROZE OVER, many townspeople skated there. We did too, but we had another place to skate – the swamp near our house. The swamp had plenty of water, but also many weeds and grasses. The boys in the neighborhood cleared the weeds from a small area to create a hockey rink. We girls would skate there when the boys were not using it. We discovered that we could skate between the weeds where a long ribbon of ice stretched. We'd skate as far as we could, then turn around and skate back, always single file.

The boys wanted more space for their games, so they pulled out more weeds. It took a long time to do that by hand. One day, they set fire to a cluster of weeds. The fire spread until the sky was blazing red. The fire trucks were blaring and rushed to the scene.

The next day, the boys saw that the fire did a good job of clearing out the weeds. After that, they set fire to the swamp every year. The firemen accepted the fact that the swamp would somehow catch fire every year. They always came.

Ruth Involved in Winter Snow Sports

The Card Games

MA AND PA LOVED TO play cards – Rummy, Hearts, Old Maid, but their favorite game was Whist, a game similar to Bridge. The game was played at our house, and the players were neighbors. There were many players, and the cast was always changing. One frequent player was Mary Boland. She was a widow whose husband had died from pneumonia. There was no penicillin to treat the disease at that time. She was left with five boys to raise. Another was old Mr. Talbott, a widower. His main topic of conversation was modern women. They wanted to work outside the home, get involved in politics and worst of all – be educated. In his view, women belong in the home cooking and cleaning. Ma and Pa believed in educating girls, but when we'd argue with him, Ma would change the subject and tell us later – leave him alone, he'll never change. Another player was Edmund Ambrozik. He was mildly retarded and very sweet. Everyone in town knew him and looked after him. He was included in all town activities.

The Whist players never made plans. They'd knock on the door in the evening and ask "Are we playing cards tonight?"

Pa was not serious about the game. He'd liven things up by cheating. He wasn't subtle about it. If he wanted his partner to play diamonds, he would point to his ring finger, for hearts, he'd put his hand on his heart, for spades, he'd simulate digging, and clubs, he'd pretend to whack the table with a club. This would make the other players angry. Many times, Mary Boland would storm home, saying "I don't play with cheaters". Edmund was very sensitive. He often went home crying if Pa told him he had played the wrong card. They'd stay away for a few days, and then return to play if Pa would agree not to cheat. Pa

would agree, and would behave for quite a while, until he again craved a little drama.

Ma was always welcoming and soothing hurt feelings. She would end the evening with a pot of tea and cookies. If everyone stayed long enough for tea and cookies, it was a happy evening.

**For all of us today's experiences
are tomorrow's memories**

The Carnival

EVERY SUMMER, WE LOOKED FORWARD to the Carnival coming to our town. The men would set up several booths in a field off Water Street and stay for a week. At one booth, we'd get three balls for a dime. We'd throw the balls, trying to knock down the three big dolls perched on a shelf on the back wall of the booth. We never saw anyone knock them down, but we'd sometimes see a young man with a huge stuffed animal, which was the prize at that booth. At another booth, we'd put our dime on a number at the front of the booth. The barker would spin a colorful steel wheel. If the wheel stopped at our number, we'd win a prize. None of us ever won, but I did win a box of chocolates at another attraction. In this area, there were several small turtles, with numbers painted on their backs. I put down my dime, and chose a number. The turtles raced as we cheered for our number. My little animal hurried past the others and crossed the finish line first. I was very happy when I was presented with a box of Whitman Samplers chocolate.

Every evening the barker would sell a bottle of brown liquid. The barker would announce that drinking this liquid would cure asthma, constipation, backaches, insomnia, rheumatism, diarrhea and a host of other problems. Most nights, an older man from town would be on the stage testifying that although he'd been drinking the tonic for a short time, he already felt much better. Every night, the barker sold many bottles of the drink.

When I think of the Carnival, I think of John Halliday. He was my boyfriend when we were 12. We'd smile at each other as we passed each other walking around the Carnival. At that time and that age, being boyfriend and girlfriend meant we'd smile or wave as we passed each other. John went to Europe during World War II and

never returned. I think of him whenever I see or read about a Carnival.

Don't hurry, don't worry.
You're only here for a short visit.
Be sure to stop and smell the flowers
(Walter Hagan)

The Vendors on Vernon Street

IN THE SUMMER, WE'D HAVE vendors going up and down Vernon Street with their horse and wagon. One was the umbrella man who called out "I'll mend your umbrella." Another was the knife and scissors man. He had a wheel on his wagon on which he sharpened knives and scissors. There was the junkman who would buy rags and metal. Ma liked the vegetable man. He sold all kinds of fruit and vegetables which he weighed on the scale he had on his truck. Ma wouldn't pay the first price he asked, she'd negotiate for several minutes. We were happy when she bought corn on the cob. The vendor would not weigh the corn, he'd just put it in a big basket. I later heard that corn is good only if you eat it the day it is picked. We never had that luxury, but we enjoyed our stale corn

With all the horses traveling along the street, the town was obliged to clean the street every evening. A town truck sprayed water along the street, and town workers shoveled debris into a truck.

There were always lots of flies and mosquitoes, but we assumed that was a natural part of the summer days.

Ruth, Pa and Dot (with Pa's pocket watch)

Clocks

WE HAD MANY CLOCK IN our house. Ma said most of them were wedding gifts. It was considered good luck to get a clock as a gift. I liked the one on the kitchen shelf. It was an ornate dignified clock about two feet tall with a carved body and a glass door. Pa would open the door once a week to wind the clock and adjust the pendulum. It had a quiet soothing ticking sound.

The clock in the dining room was a beautiful mantle clock of black and gold. It had two pillars on each side of the clock face. This clock never had the correct time. It was strictly ornamental. Another clock I remember is the Big Ben. Pa had it in his bedroom and wound it every night. It ticked so loudly that I didn't know how Ma and Pa could sleep, but they did.

Once, Pa painted the kitchen. He took down the old shelf and put up a new one. The clock was too tall for the new shelf. Pa must have been in a hurry, because instead of moving the shelf, he cut the top off that wonderful clock.

At that time, not many had watches but Pa did. It was a gold watch on a chain which he wore on his vest. One Sunday he wore it when we went to the Common. Somehow it fell off. We all spent hours searching for it, but never found it. Pa was heartbroken as this was his one Treasure.

Few people had wrist watches then. They must have been very expensive. My brother and sisters got a wrist-watch as a gift when they graduated from High School.

When I asked Ma why I didn't get one, she said, "We sent you to college instead."

I did get a wristwatch for my 28th birthday, a gift from my husband, Chuck. I've had many wristwatches since, but I loved the first one, and kept it for many years.

Stockings

UNTIL THE 1960'S, WOMEN SELDOM wore pants. Therefore, stockings were important and there was always the problem – how to hold them up. As children, we wore knee socks and garters. The older women wore corsets which had garters attached, the younger women wore garter belts. The flappers wore round garters.

During the cold Massachusetts winters, we wore long underwear under our stockings. Some people, like Dot, could fold the underwear neatly under their stockings. Others, like Ruth, had lumpy legs all winter.

When we were young women, we had silk stocking when we dressed up. These stockings had a seam up the back. We'd always ask "Is my seam straight?"

During World War II, nylons were invented. Every woman wanted a pair. If we heard that a store had them for sale, we'd rush to the store. Nylons were a popular gift for a sailor or soldier to give his girlfriend.

Mary had a machine that mended runs in the nylons. It took a steady hand and patience which Mary had.

During the summer months, we'd often put a liquid tan makeup on to cover our white legs. Ma didn't like that at all, as often we didn't take time to wash our legs thoroughly before going to bed – of course the sheets were stained.

One evening, Kay and I went to a USO swim party at the Charlestown YMCA. Kay put on her bathing suit. She

had applied the makeup only up to her knees. I laughed and Kay did too, eventually, when she saw her white thighs about the make-up.

When pants became stylish, we no longer worried about how to hold up those stockings.

Ruth and Katie with Friends

The Summer Pajamas

WHEN KAY WAS IN HIGH school, colorful summer pajamas were in style. They were adorned with bright flowers or birds, had wide graceful legs. They were lovely. Many of her friends had a pair, and, of course, Kay wanted them. She talked to Ma about her problem, but Ma said, "I'm sorry, but we don't have extra money right now." Kay was undaunted. She determined to earn the money. Since this was during the depression, jobs were scarce. She applied at all the stores in town, but no one was hiring. She tried to get a baby-sitting job, but that failed. Kay then realized that the only way she could earn money was by selling blueberries. She'd pick early in the morning, come home dirty and tired, clean up and gallantly go out to sell them. She endured rejection as, even the 25 cents a quart, was more than many people could afford. Eventually, she had the money she needed for the object of her desire. She wore them almost every day for the rest of the summer. To us, she looked like a glamorous movie star in the pajamas.

Even Ma thought they were beautiful. She admired Kay's persistence in getting what she wanted.

Kay and Bill

The Moonlight Girls

WHEN WE WERE YOUNG, THE girls in the neighborhood would stroll down Vernon Street, singing the latest songs. A local store sold song sheets so we knew all the words. One of our favorite songs was "Moonlight Bay". Kay and her girlfriends Mary Morgan and Mary Sweeney like it because they could harmonize while singing it. We thought they should be on the radio, but that never happened. We started calling the three girls "The Moonlight Girls". They liked being singled out as special. They then decided to have secret meetings, opened only to "Moonlight Girls". The meetings were held in a shed in Mary Sweeney's yard. I don't know what went on at these meetings, but I suspect that its purpose was to exclude all but the three Moonlight Girls.

They soon inducted other girls into their secret society but never me and Dot.

Moonlight Bay

We were sailing along
On Moonlight Bay
We could hear the darkies singing
They seemed to say
You have stolen my heart
Now don't go away
As we sing love's old sweet song
On Moonlight Bay.

Live your life and forget your age

The Red Wagon

IT WAS 5:00 P.M. AND Bill was at the factory gate of the Hollywood Wakefield Furniture Factory. He was selling newspapers out of his red wagon to the men leaving work. He did this every week day. If Bill was sick, Mary substituted, although reluctantly. Bill was only 12, but was already a hard worker.

Bill's red wagon was important to the family as we had no car. If anything heavy or bulky needed to be delivered, Bill and his red wagon were dispatched. If we ran out of ice, Bill and his wagon went to the ice house for more.

Bill enjoyed going around town on errands at a young age. But he was possessive of his wagon. He didn't want anyone else pulling it.

Mary had a red scooter –that was just for fun.

Diseases of the Time

IN THE 1920'S AND 1930'S, many contagious diseases spread through the community. There was no cure for these diseases – Diptheria, Scarlet Fever, Measles, Whopping Cough, and Pneumonia. If a neighbor developed one of these dread diseases, all would be concerned. A classmate of mine lost two sisters to Scarlet Fever. If someone had one of these diseases, an official from the town health department would put a quarantine sign on the house. This was a warning for people to stay out, to prevent the spread of the disease.

We Joyce's had the usual childhood diseases, measles, mumps, and chicken pox. As an infant, I almost died of whooping cough. Bill had T.B. and was sent to a sanitarium for one year. The treatment for T.B. was fresh air and sunshine. It worked for Bill as he lived to be 96.

In the 1950's, the dreaded polio appeared. Many died; many could not breathe on their own, and would live in an iron lung. Some were left paralyzed or with a limp. One evening, our neighbors, Tom and Carol Kelly offered to babysit while Chuck and I went to the movies. We jumped at the change – a rare treat. When we returned, Tom greeted us with the news that Carol had been taken to the hospital with polio. We watched and worried about our children. They were fine as was Carol. She had a mild case. A few years later, Dr. Jonas Salk discovered a vaccine to prevent polio. He was a hero to us all.

Molasses

MOLASSES WAS AN IMPORTANT PART of our diet in Boston. Ma used it in making her gingerbread and gingersnaps. Our favorite snack was the sweet, sticky liquid spread on white bread. Every Saturday, Ma would make a big crock of baked beans with molasses and bacon. We'd have it for dinner with brown bread. The odor was enticing and the taste delicious. Pa would say "Save some for my Sunday breakfast". Then he'd tell us about the molasses flood in the North end of Boston a few years prior. A massive molasses tank broke, spilling thick sticky liquid all over the neighborhood. It destroyed homes and killed several people. Does anybody eat molasses anymore?

Hot Chocolate

WHEN WE WERE YOUNG, WE loved a snow storm. It looked beautiful decorating the tree branches and we'd have no school. But, best of all, we could go sledding. We lived at the bottom of a hill. Highland Street was the best street in the neighborhood for sledding. As a result, lots of children would come to our street.

We could not steer the sled and it had no brakes. To protect ourselves from running into the street in the path of a car, we'd post someone near the street to signal when it was safe.

One day when we'd been playing a while and were wet, cold and hungry, Ma invited me and three friends into the house for hot chocolate. We sat at the dining room table and drank the hot chocolate from Ma's beautiful fragile hot chocolate set. We felt like Princesses holding the dainty cups. I had admired them in Ma's china cabinet but this was the first time I was allowed to drink from them. The beverage tasted delicious from the delicate cups. After Ma washed them, she put them back in the china cabinet to be seen but seldom used.

Life is like a box of chocolates (Forrest Gump)

The Blueberry Picnic

EVERY SUMMER, OUR FAMILY WOULD go on a blueberry picnic. Ma would pack a lunch, and we'd all walk to the Rifle Range. There were lots of blueberries there. We'd hear gun shots, which were frightening to me, but Ma assured us that we were safe. Ma would make pies with some of the berries; the rest, we children could sell and keep the money. My big sister, Mary, who was quite bossy, reminded me of Ma's rule "Sell to strangers, but don't bother Ma's friends." I hated that rule, approaching strangers meant rejection. When Mary was away, I sneaked downtown Mrs. Conway's house. As I expected, she said "You're one of the Joyce girls; I'll buy your berries." The truth surfaced eventually, but I had my money, and Ma forgave me.

Pa, Mary and Dot

Pa and Eggs

PA THOUGHT EGGS WERE THE perfect food. He ate one every morning for the breakfast, usually soft boiled in a white egg cup. We had lots of egg cups in many colors, but the white one was his. He would peel the shell from the top of the egg, salt it, then break the egg with his spoon, spilling the yellow down the egg cup. Paying no attention to the mess he was making, he'd enjoy his egg. If we were sick, he'd suggest we eat an egg. When we were older, he'd say "Have you had your egg today?"

My sister, Mary, didn't like eggs and refused to ever eat one. Pa worried about her and was certain she wouldn't live long. Mary lived a long and healthy life. Her death at age 89 had nothing at all to do with a lack of eggs in her diet.

Pa, you're the best and at the top of my list;
just in case I never let you know,
with all my whole heart I love you so

The Iceman

IT WAS A HAPPY DAY for our family. Tomorrow, our first electric refrigerator was to be delivered. It would be placed in the kitchen, not down cellar with the ice chest. I was sad. I'd miss the iceman. Mother would put the card in the window, letting the iceman know how big a piece of ice we wanted. The iceman was friendly and strong. Donning a rubber apron, he'd hoist the heavy ice cube with tongs and haul it to the cellar. When he was leaving, we'd gather around his wagon, hoping to get a sliver of ice wrapped in newspaper, as a treat. Sometimes he'd let us pet his horse. The ice age was ending.

The Hurricane

IT WAS A WINDY DAY in September, 1938. The wind got stronger and stronger until Ma called us to get into the house. The radio reported that it was a hurricane, a rare event in our area. We watched in amazement from indoors – tree branches were falling, roofs were torn from our neighbor's houses. We had an apple tree in the back yard which was swaying back and forth. If it went one way, it would fall on the houses. It must have been very flexible as it swayed and bent but never fell. The next day, Dot and I walked around. It was astonishing what damage had been done in a short time. The streets were full of trees, branches, pieces of roofs, chairs, tables blown from porches. The damage at the ocean side was much worse. Houses tumbled into the ocean, boats crumbled and lives were lost. We realized that we can't control Mother Nature.

Ruth and Pa

Boston

BOSTON WAS TO ME A magical city. It was exciting to see so many people, all in a hurry, all well-dressed. I felt lucky when Ma took me shopping in Boston. We'd walk to the train station in Wakefield, and then take a train to the North Station. From there, we'd walk to Raymonds. Raymonds was a discount store before there were discount stores. It was full of goods – clothes, blankets, tablecloths, but Mother went first to the corset department. In those days, all the women wore corsets. The corsets had four garters attached to them. They were used to hold up the women's stockings. Pantyhose had not yet been invented. There was an array of corsets to choose from; all with numerous strings to make them adjustable. Our next stop was Filenes, where we'd go directly to the basement which was a treasure trove. There were quality clothes at a low price. Most of the clothes were from Neiman Marcus, according to the sign in the store. Unfortunately, Filenes had no dressing rooms at the time. The customers had to guess if the garment would fit or peel off as many layers as they dared, then try the clothes on. We'd see women in all stages of undress, more concerned with getting a bargain than retaining their modesty. We'd then walk to Jordan Marsh. I liked the ambiance at Jordan's. The smell of perfume would greet you at the door. Their candy counter was amazing. We'd buy candy to take home.

My favorite store was Kresge's. It was noisy, crowded and filled with the scent of popcorn and hot dogs. Ma and I would sit at the lunch counter, and have a hot dog and root beer for seven cents. It always tasted delicious, maybe because we were very hungry by then. We'd then start for home, loaded with packages, and tired from so much walking. For me, it was always a good day.

Christmas

LIKE ALL CHILDREN, WE LOVED Christmas. We'd hang up our stocking on Christmas Eve, not a fancy Christmas stocking, but one of our everyday ones. In the morning we'd find apples, oranges and walnuts in them. Bill always got a lump of coal. I think Ma and Pa thought since he was a boy, he must have done something bad. Bill didn't seem to mind. He knew he'd get presents as well. We girls never got coal. If we had, our sobs would have broken the peace of Christmas morning.

On Christmas Eve, we'd go to bed early. I'd hear Santa's bells ringing, but I wouldn't get out of bed. Could it have been Pa ringing the bells? We'd get up early to look for our presents. We'd get board games, dolls, sports equipment usually two or three gifts each. There'd often be a small crisis like the time I got a dainty tea set. Carrying it to the kitchen, I fell and broke a cup. Of course, I cried and wailed. It was just a minor problem in a large family. After attending church, Ma would cook a delicious dinner: usually roast chicken, mashed potatoes and beans. After dinner, we'd visit our friends to see their gifts.

There was one gift that I looked forward to each year. It was a small box of hard candy from our Sunday school teacher. I didn't often have that much candy all for myself. No wonder we loved Christmas.

The Christmas Tree

EVERY CHRISTMAS EVE, PA AND his five children would wander around town from one Christmas tree lot to another looking for a well-shaped tree for 25 cents – that's all Pa was willing to pay. If we found one for 50 cents, Pa would say "It's too tall" or "One side is bare". Then Pa would find one he liked. If we pointed out its flaws – it's crooked – it has a bare spot, Pa would say "It just needs attention", and attention it would get. Pa would drill holes on the bare side, then take branches from the full side and put them in the holes he had drilled. We'd all give orders to Pa – put a branch here, put the bare side against the wall.

Pa would listen and alter the tree. When he was finished, we thought it was beautiful especially when we added ornaments and lights.

The lights were on a string. If one light went out, they all went out. We'd have to test them all to find the bad one and replace it. This took lots of my time during the Christmas season. Since I was the youngest, I was meant for this menial chore according to my sisters.

Ma and Bill

Easter

AFTER A LONG, COLD SNOWY winter New Englanders looked forward to warm weather and spring finery. In those days, everyone wore hats, not just for Sunday, but every day. I still remember the pretty pink hat I wore on my first day of school. If times were good, Ma would get us new hats. If not, we'd wear our old hats, and scurry to seven o'clock mass to avoid the fashion parade at the ten o'clock mass.

Ma made us dresses when we were young. She always made me bloomers to match my dresses with a pocket for my handkerchief. Ma made sure we all had a clean handkerchief when we went to school. There were no Kleenex tissues then. I don't know why the pocket was in the bloomers instead of in the dress. Ma wanted us to look good; neat was the word she used. She wouldn't say "You look pretty" but "You look neat".

Every year, the school took our pictures, and sent copies home with us. The photographer hoped the parents would buy them. Ma never did. One year, Bill's picture was not at all neat. He had on his heavy outside sweater, sleeves rolled up, with his long-sleeved white shirt hanging to his wrist. Ma was angry. "I told you to take that heavy sweater off in school" she said. After that she reminded him every day "Take that sweater off in school".

We girls were fashion-conscious and tried to dress well. Kay went a little further and tried to look different. She'd wear a scarf as a belt to brighten an old dress. One day, she wore her pajama top with a skirt. Mary, who was quite conservative, said "You're not wearing that to school, are you?" Kay just said "Yes" and she did.

Bill and all the boys all wore knickers. They wore short pants with a buckle at the knee to tighten them. He wore fancy long socks with them. When the boys were twelve, they graduated to long pants. Women and girls never wore pants.

When I was going to college, Ma took me clothes shopping. She liked the plaid dress with the white Peter Pan collar. I liked the sophisticated navy blue dress. Ma bought both. Having two new dresses was an unexpected treat.

When Mary, Kay and Dot worked in Boston they got most of their dresses in Filene's Basement which sold high quality clothes at a low cost. It was difficult to dress well on a small budget but it was fun trying.

On Easter, Ma bought us each an Easter egg. We never had Easter baskets. The egg was the size of a hen's egg and had a chicken or bunny on top. The egg was so hard that we couldn't bite it. We'd suck it, it was very sweet. It would last at least a week. Ma made a big ham dinner for Easter and a homemade cake.

Easter was a religious holiday, but we also celebrated warm weather and spring clothes.

Ruth in her Hawaiian Outfit

Memorial Day

EVERY MEMORIAL DAY, ALMOST EVERYONE in town would visit the cemetery. We'd walk to St. Patrick's Cemetery in Stoneham where Claire was buried. Claire was Ruth's twin sister who died when she was two months old. Pa made a white wooden cross every year for Claire's grave. Pa would carry the cross, Ma would carry a lunch, and Mary would carry a pot of flowers. As we walked along Albion Street, there were so many people going that way, that it was almost a parade. We'd place the cross and the flowers on Claire's grave, and say some prayers. The adults would visit, and we children would find friends to talk to until lunchtime.

There would be a priest to say Mass, but that took place early in the morning, before we got to the cemetery.

Ma's friend, Mary Boland, was a widow. She met John, a widower, whose wife was buried in the plot next to Mary's husband. They dated for a long time, but Mary didn't want marriage. Mary had five boys. The youngest son, Richard, wanted the marriage to take place as the potential groom had promised Richard a pony if he could convince his mother to marry John. He couldn't convince his mother to marry John. He never got his pony.

It was a sad time for the adults thinking of their lost loved ones, but the children were not too sad. Claire had died so young, that we hardly knew her. I often think how wonderful it would be to have a twin sister, but I'm grateful I had Mary, Kay, Dot and also Bill.

**God gave us memories so that we
might have roses in December**

The Movies

WHEN WE WERE YOUNG, WE'D like to spend Saturday afternoon at the movies. If Ma didn't have the dime we needed, she'd say, "Go down to the cellar and see if there are any bottles you can cash". Each bottle brought five cents, so we needed only two bottle caps.

The movie would be a double feature usually including one cowboy story. Tom Mix was our favorite. We'd also see newsreels, coming attractions, and a serial. The serial would be an action packed drama where the Hero would be pursued by very ornery villains from whom there was no escape. Sometimes the Heroine would be in trouble. She'd be in the window of a burning building from which there was no escape. When the action was at its most dramatic, the words would come across the screen "To Be Continued". Our creativity would be stirred, as we'd discuss solutions for the hero and heroine. We'd want to go the next Saturday to see how the hero did escape. Sometimes the escape was miraculous.

The movies were a wonderful source of entertainment and discussion.

Prohibition

IN THE EARLY 1900'S, A group of hard working, politically active women realized that many social ills such as domestic abuse, unemployment and homelessness were caused by alcohol. They called themselves "The Women's Christian Temperance Union". These women traveled around the country preaching the evils of liquor. They persuaded Congress to pass the 18th amendment which prohibited the manufacture and sale of alcoholic beverages.

Canada, however, was still producing and selling alcohol, so bootleggers smuggled it into the United States. Many of them became very wealthy. Speakeasies flourished. These were restaurants that sold liquor illegally. The owners would frequently bribe the police to avoid being raided. Of course, the men from small towns like Wakefield couldn't get to the big city speak easies. They made their own home brew.

Pa made home brew in the basement. He had a machine which put the caps on the bottles.

One evening, we all went to visit our neighbor, the Murphys. Mr. Murphy had his home brew in the kitchen. I leaned over the pot and a terrible thing happened: my hat fell in. Pa grabbed my hat and screamed. Mr. Murphy screamed louder. My sweet Pa called me names he'd never used before – "dumb, silly, crazy, and stupid". No one cared about my almost new red hat. Pa forgave me the next day. It took Mr. Murphy a little longer.

In 1933, Congress passed the 21st amendment, which repealed the 18th amendment. After thirteen years, we could again manufacture and sell liquor.

Pa was glad when that happened. He said the commercial beer tasted much better than home brew.

The Great Depression

THE GREAT DEPRESSION WAS A sad time for our Nation. Thousands of men could not find jobs, resulting in widespread poverty. In Wakefield, it was made worse when the Heywood Wakefield Furniture Factory moved to Gardner, Mass, two hours north of Wakefield. Many families moved to Gardner. Others, like Pa, worked all week in Gardner and came home weekends. We all wrote Pa letters as we knew he was lonesome. Pa worked in Gardner for several months, but after paying room, board, and transportation, he had little money left. He decided to come home and find a job in Wakefield. He applied for work at all the factories and stores. No one was hiring. Finally Ma and Pa made the difficult decision to apply for welfare. Ma was quite upset. At that time, there were no federal welfare programs, but the town of Wakefield tried to help its residents. We were given a food voucher to use at a store where we had never shopped. The town selectmen wanted to help all the merchants, so they all got food voucher customers. We were never hungry. Ma was a good cook and could stretch the food. However, we seldom had dessert. One Sunday, our relatives from Boston visited us. All their visits were unannounced as we had no phone. Ma always served them tea and cookies. That day there were only enough cookies for the guests, so we children were warned not to take any cookies. After that, Ma kept a box of cookies hidden in the living room closet away from her five hungry children.

Before long, we needed shoes. We were given vouchers at a certain shoe store. That year, Brown shoes were in style. The store had brown shoes in my size, but only black in my sister's sizes. Mary moaned "Black shoes, everyone

will know they're welfare shoes." We didn't want our friends to know we were on welfare.

We had very few clothes, but Ma did laundry every day, so we were always clean and neat. We couldn't afford new dresses, so we took care of the ones we had. We mended, altered, dyed, added ribbons or buttons – did anything to make the dresses look new and different. I had a pink dress that was faded and too short. I dyed it green and added a plaid taffeta ribbon along the hem line. It looked great. Dot had a plaid skirt and blouse that was badly faded. She carefully took it apart at the seams, reversed it so that the unfaded inside was now on the out-side. It looked like a new dress.

We couldn't buy new socks, so we darned the old ones. We had a wooden egg with a handle. We'd put the egg into the heel of the sock and darn. If you darned well, it was hardly noticeable, but if you didn't do it well, you'd have a lump in your heel and soon, a blister.

Pa was in charge of shoe repairs. In the cellar, he had several different size shoe lasts. He'd put one on his metal pedestal, and then put the shoe on, sole side up, and he was ready to work. Woolworth's store sold shoe repair kits which consisted of glue and rubber to attach to a worn sole. We kept our shoes well-polished possibly to hide the fact that our shoes were old and worn.

Since we couldn't buy much of anything new, Pa was always fixing up and patching around the house.

Our house had only one children's book "The Tale of Peter Rabbit" which someone had given to Mary. We did have a wonderful library in town– The Lucius Beebe Memorial Library. There was an adult library and a chil-

dren's library. I spent a lot of time at the library, not only for books but to meet my friends and visit, much to the annoyance of the librarian.

At home, we played card games, checkers, and listened to the radio.

Ma and Pa never spent money on themselves, we children came first. We were always at the dentist, but Ma and Pa never went, even though their teeth needed attention.

During the depression, Ma and Pa were concerned that they'd lose their house as many people did. However, the bank was understanding and allowed them to pay a small amount toward the mortgage each month.

Sometime later, Pa got a job as a laborer for the town. It was not the job he dreamed of, but it got us off welfare.

While sweeping and cleaning around town, Pa would find pieces of metal which he's save. When he had a bagful, he'd take them to Mr. Levine, our local junkman, who bought them. After that, Pa always carried a magnet so he could judge if the metal was iron or brass.

Many years later, Bill worked at Evan Shoe Factory, and Mary worked at the Harvard Knitting Mills. They both lived at home, and contributed to the household expenses. When we had enough money saved, we decided to turn the pantry into a bathroom. We were happy about that —- lots of hot water would be a treat. But Kay didn't think so – she wanted to buy a car. "Think of all we can see and do in a car – not in a bathroom." Kay loved adventure.

She eventually joined the Coast Guard to help the war effort and to see the world. She got to Pittsburgh, Pa.

In 1941, our country went to war. That was another terrible time for our country, but it did end the depression. There were lots of jobs in the war industries.

Pa, Ruth, Bill and Dot

Jobs, Jobs, Jobs

DURING THE DEPRESSION, THE LUCKY people were the ones who had a job, any job. The specter of being unemployed haunted people. As a result, whenever we girls brought a boyfriend home, Ma would ask "Does he have a job?"

We all worked as soon as we were sixteen. Bill had his paper route, and we girls worked in the local stores, Woolworth, Kresge, Neisners, and Grants. When Bill graduated from high school, he was hired at Evans Shoe Factory in Wakefield. Mary, Kay and Dot had secretarial jobs in Boston. Because I went to college, I had four years of various jobs in the summer and on Saturdays.

One store job I had was at the A&P grocery store in the produce department. It had always been a young man's job, but this was wartime. The young men were in the service. Three girls were hired – Jane, Mary and Ruth. We had the same duties as the young men before us – hauling heavy sacks of potatoes, apples, onions and other vegetables and fruits up from the basement, arranging the fruits and vegetables neatly, removing bad fruit, and selling to the customers. Often, at this time, certain foods would be in scarce supply. Ma and her friends would be understanding. It was for God and Country. However, when potatoes were scarce, it was different. As Pa said, "A dinner without potatoes is not a dinner at all". However, Ma had a solution for her friends – ask Ruth. She was sure that the basement of the A&P was full of potatoes but not so. Ruth would suggest squash, turnip, beets, but the women always left unhappy without potatoes.

Pa thought a Civil Service job was great. The pay was good, and the work steady. Every day, Pa would scan the newspaper for announcements of a Civil Service test. If he found one was being conducted in Boston, Dot, Mary, Kay and I would take a train to Boston, and then find our way by subway or the El (elevated subway) to the school where the test was held. If we did well on the test, we'd be offered a job. Sometimes, the job was too far away to be practical. But I did get a job at the Department of Motor Vehicles. I spent the day filing papers. I actually found a stolen car through paper work.

Almost everyone in the neighborhood worked at Paul Guillows Airplane factory, packaging balsa wood air planes. Paul would be in the field next to the factory, testing new models. We sat at long wooden benches with no backs. We had no coffee breaks, no lunch room. There was one thing the women liked about working there. Paul would allow them to work whenever they could. Many worked while their children were in school. This practice was unusual then.

I had many waitress jobs. I spent one summer working in a hotel in the White Mountains of New Hampshire.

The most memorable waitress job was at Sailor Tom's in North Reading. This was a popular seafood restaurant in North Reading known for its fried clams and french fries. Sailor Tom was a burly, rough hard working retired sailor. He hired other retired sailors to work in the kitchen. They were hard working but had a weakness for liquor. There was always someone in the kitchen who had beer or another drink. When tensions got high, the knives would fly. Many times, an ambulance would take a knife victim to the hospital. He'd be back soon, patched up and ready to work. Luckily, no one in that part of the country had guns.

Tom's wife, Polly was a tall, strong, confident woman. She was always in the dining room to make sure that the waitresses were safe, the customers were unaware of the mayhem in the kitchen, and no one left without paying his bill. I was eventually promoted to cashier. That was easier than waitressing, and I liked dressing up. When the restaurant closed for the night, I had to balance the cash in the register and the register tape. I always had my eye on the clock, as I didn't want to miss the last bus to Wakefield. No one in the family had a car, so I'd be in trouble if I missed that bus – I never did.

Sailor Tom had a soft side. He'd buy a wheelchair for anyone who needed one. He'd raise the money for the chairs anyway he could. One time, for 25 cents, the waitresses were allowed to see his appendectomy scar. We were intimidated and all paid that 25 cents and saw that ugly scar.

During the war, everyone worked. It was the patriotic thing to do. Women, who had never worked outside the home, worked in defense plants. Many people worked at their regular jobs all day and at a defense plant at night. I was hired at Standard Brands Factory where I filled tea bags for iced tea for the navy. That did not last long as I got a rash from the tea dust. I then found work soldering radio boxes for the Navy. Several of us sat at long tables. It was crowded and noisy but I liked it. I was eventually promoted to Inspector.

During the war, women discovered that they were smart and competent. They could do difficult and technical jobs that were formerly done only by men. The war changed women and the men who lived with them.

F.D.R.

IN THE 1930'S, WE WERE in the middle of a depression. There was widespread unemployment. The banks failed. Ma's brother had saved enough money for a trip to Ireland, but lost it in the bank crash. Al Smith, the Governor of New York, ran for President against Herbert Hoover. Al Smith was a catholic, so, of course, we favored him. We'd sing "East side, west side, all around the town, we'll put Hoover in a box and turn him upside down". Hoover won the presidency. He was, in our opinion, not good looking, charming, or a persuasive speaker. He was defeated by Franklin Delano Roosevelt in 1933. A baby living on Highland Street was the first baby in the nation born after FDR's inauguration. The baby received a letter from FDR, souvenirs, and lots of publicity. His parents named him Franklin.

Roosevelt set to work improving the economy, with programs known by their initials: WPA was Works Progress Administration. Pa worked on WPA, repairing roads. The CCC was the Civilian Conservation Corps, formed to address the problem of unemployed young men. They lived in camps around the country. They built and repaired parks and recreation areas. These boys had lived in poverty and were now given good food and lodging in exchange for hard work. We had a CCC camp between the towns of Wakefield and Saugus. It was called Wake-Sau. It became a large park with a playground, swimming pools, picnic area, and hiking trails. It is still there and is a popular place for recreation activities.

Mary and Bill

The War Years

ON SUNDAY, DECEMBER 7, 1941, THE whole family was listening to the radio, as our President, Franklin D. Roosevelt, declared war on Japan. The Japanese had bombed Pearl Harbor. We were surprised and shocked. We were concerned about all the young men who would be conscripted into the Army.

Bill was one of the first men to go. Ma never cried, but the night before Bill left, Ma sobbed and sobbed. She was sure she'd never see him again. Bill was away for four years; in many locations in the States and even in France. Luckily, he was never in combat.

The War Years were dark and gloomy. We would oftern have blackouts, when no lights were allowed. Volunteer Air Raid Wardens would scan the sky with binoculars searching for enemy planes.

The home front was deeply involved in the war effort. Every able bodied man and woman worked including many women who had never worked outside the home. It was the patriotic thing to do. Many worked regular jobs, and worked nights at a War Industry.

Many foods were rationed – meat, cheese, coffee. We were issued coupon books for the rationed food. If the rationed food became available, lines would form to buy them. Gas was also rationed.

People were encouraged to plant Victory Gardens. Pa dug up our back yard so we could plant vegetables.

The War years were especially difficult for the Mothers. The young men were drafted and sent away – nobody knew where. The young men would write letters home, but if they indicated where they were stationed, the information was cut out of the letters. The saying was: "Loose lips sink ships".

A banner with a blue star was displayed in the window of a house that was home to a serviceman. If one had died, the star was gold.

Our local weekly newspaper listed the names of servicemen who had been injured or died. It was sad, since we knew most of them.

The war in Europe was over on May 7, 1945. The war with Japan was over on September 2, 1945. That was one month after President Harry Truman dropped an atomic bomb on Hiroshima, Japan. Everyone celebrated – horns blasting, dancing in the streets. The war was over, at last.

Dot and Bill

U.S.O. (United Service Organization)

DURING THE WAR, THERE WERE no men around for us to date. They were all in the services. In Boston, many place had U.S.O. dances. We'd go there when we could to dance and talk with the servicemen. Most of them were lonesome, and wanted to talk about home.

At one dance, a good looking sailor asked me to dance. I then introduced him to my sisters. He was interested in Mary. She was very pretty with black hair, white skin and beautiful elbows. Whenever he could, he would call her and meet her. He came to Wakefield to meet the family. Joe was falling in love with Mary. We all liked him, but Pa was unhappy when he married Mary and took her so far away, to Buffalo.

Mary's Wedding on May 25, 1946

MARY WAS THE FIRST ONE in the family to get married in 1947. That morning, in the house, it was chaos. One bathroom and seven people trying to get ready for an early morning wedding was difficult. Since we had no car, we arranged for the neighborhood men with cars to transport us to the church. The first car was for Mary, the bride, Kay, the bridesmaid and Ma. The second car was for Pa, Ruth and Dot. The third car was for Bill, who was the best man, Joe, the groom and the ushers.

The first car started just as Kay was descending the steps to the street. Kay stood in the middle of Vernon Street in her bridesmaid finery, yelling at the departing car "What the hell kind of wedding is this?" Dot and Ruth joined Kay in yelling at the driver until he returned for Kay. Now, Dot and Ruth had to take care of Pa. He was sitting in his car with his feet on the ground sobbing "Why is Mary going so far away? We'll never see her". Dot was saying "Stop crying. You can't cry at the wedding". Ruth was saying "It is a sad day for you Pa". When he couldn't stop, Ruth went down to the cellar where Pa kept his liquor, poured some whiskey in a glass, added water and gave it to Pa. He drank it and soon felt better.

We got through the beautiful ceremony. The reception was held in a restaurant in Lynnfield where there was lots of singing and dancing.

Mary came to visit us frequently after her marriage. Ma and Pa got to stay a few weeks in Depew every year, where Mary and Joe lived. They enjoyed the beauties of the area including Niagara Falls.

Pa, Bill, Joe, Mary and Kay on Mary and Joe's Wedding Day

Whether a family is bound together or scattered far apart, loved ones from the past and the present are always in our heart

We're Irish You Know

PA WOULD ALWAYS TELL US that the Irish girls were the prettiest; the Irish boys were the best fighters. Pa like boxing.

According to Pa, the Irish are musical and great dancers. He informed us that when he was young, he was the best dancer in Ireland. In the evening, Pa would teach us the Irish Jig. Mary was very good at it. If we weren't doing well, Pa would say with derision "You don't know a jig from a reel".

Ma and Pa would often recite poetry which they had learned in school in Ireland.
"Hark, hark the dogs do bark, the beggars are coming to town."
"The boy stood on the burning deck whenst all but he had fled."

We would promise to take Pa to Ireland, but he'd say "No, America is much better. I don't want to go to Ireland." We are all glad that Ma and Pa came to America.

In 1999, Mary, Dot and Ruth visited Ma's relatives in Ireland. Stephen McWalter, Ma's sister's son, lives on the family farm where Ma grew up. His brother, Patrick McWalter, lives nearby. The relatives were very welcoming. Mary Dolan, who is Stephen and Patrick's sister, is the only one we're still in touch with. She lives with her daughter in a two story house which is unusual in that area. Her address is:

Mrs. Mary Dolan
Lissarvally
Barnaderg
Tuam
County Galway
Ireland

Joan, Missy, Ruth, Dot and Mary in Ireland in 1999

Appendix

Memories of My Childhood
Written by Catherine (Kay) Garvin
(Date unknown)

WE GIRLS SLEPT FOUR IN one room with one dresser to share between us and one closet for our clothes. We spent very little time in our rooms... it was a place to sleep and get dressed.

We ate very well and our mother didn't work outside the home. She cooked big meals every day such as roast beef, hams, whole chickens and on Friday a baked haddock about two feet long. She made homemade bread once a week and when we got home from school, the smell was delicious. She made several puddings which in today's restaurants would cost about $4.00 a serving.

We were taught to do well in school and I was afraid to come home with even a mark of "C". I always liked school and did well but I think school is harder for today's children. I see this when I watch my grandchildren's studies.

We made our own entertainment such as swimming in the lake and going to the playground in the summer. I remember every year at the playground there was a freckle contest where the person with the most freckles would

receive a prize. I had tons of freckles and my girlfriends and siblings insisted I enter as the prize was a box of chocolates. I won for few years in a row. My self-esteem took several years after that to emerge!!

In the winter we skated in the swamp ponds. The boys in the neighborhood used to set fires to swamps to clear the stumps. We would wait and watch for the fire department to come and put the fires out. There were two ponds and girls were sent to one to skate while the boys took the best one to play hockey. One of the local boys there made it to the Olympics.

We were walkers in those days —- no cars in families and we would walk to surrounding towns like Stoneham and Melrose to attend some activity. Walking around the lake or at least half-way was a regular thing.

I loved to roller skate and after high school when we had a little money I would go to Revere Beach to roller skate with my neighbor girlfriends. It took two bus changes to get there and we always hoped for a ride home with a guy who had a car. When one of us got an offer, the rest of would appear at the end of the night and hop in the car; the guy never had a chance!

There were no bars or liquor stores in Wakefield when I was a child. Our father made his own home brew. The word got around and we would get visitors in the evening from local drinkers looking for beer. Our mother sometimes heard them coming down the street and would put lights out, lock the door and tell us all to be quiet. It was hard to get rid of them once they got their foot in the door.

We had one fellow – I call him the educated drunk and some of us got a kick out of him when he came to the house. He would line us kids up for a spelling bee and also test us on the State Capitals. To this day I am a very good on the State Capitals when questions about them are on Jeopardy or another quiz program.

We had demoralizing transportation problems as we were older and went to Boston to dances, etc. We had to leave the dance by 11:00 pm to connect with a bus for Wakefield (the last one). I missed it on several occasions and I was locked out. When I woke my father, I was given a sound wack on the ass before I was let into the house.

The Joyce girls were into "Women's Lib" before their time and as I look back, we were not too happy about it. When our father decided that some work had to be done around the house, there was no discrimination. I remember one time I was told to get out onto a roof to install a storm window and did so without flinching!!! When a room had to be wallpapered the girls had to pitch in. The irony of it was that we were all out of high school and most of us were working —— no difference. And this was on a Saturday or a Sunday!

An incident I remember is when I climbed an apple tree in the back yard to pick apples and an apple fell when I was picking and hit Ma and she had a black eye for days. Trees were later blown down in a bad hurricane; I choose to forget that year!

We had relatives of Pa's from Lawrence that used to visit at least once a year I learned later they were just his old neighbors from County Mayo in Ireland. A mix of them would come and we would listen to them talking and laughing about Ireland. The younger element were bright, prosperous businessmen of the community and liked Pa. He would hold Court as the saying goes and enjoyed their visits. We would get invited to the Lawrence weddings and Pa would introduce his comely daughters to the prosperous Lawrence group but nothing happened as a result. We were younger than they were and apparently shy at the time!!!

Pa collected junk as another sibling stated during WW2 times. I remember helping him pile it at times in the back yard – no choice there. Humiliation of this duty didn't enter my mind at the time. It seems as Pa made equal amounts of money collecting junk as his regular salary with the Town.

As kids on Sunday, we would take a walk to the next town of Stoneham to the cemetery where Ruth's twin Claire was buried. On the way home we would stop for ice cream and visit friends that had children our age. That was our Sunday treat – yee of other generations remember this.

As siblings, we will all have some of the same memories so excuse any repetition.

Salutatory

By Mary Joyce

Walt Whitman,
Singer of American Democracy

Friends of the Class of 1933:

IT IS MY PLEASANT DUTY as spokesman for the class
of 1933 to welcome you to our commencement activities.
We doubly appreciate your cooperation with us in a year of
doubts and perplexities. Since our hearts are filled with
gratitude for the educational opportunities given to us, we
have decided to express our appreciation by a program
lauding our country. With that purpose in mind, our exer-
cises this evening are modeled upon Katherine Lee Bates's
significant poem, America the Beautiful:

> O beautiful for spacious skies
> For amber waves of grain,
> For purple mountain majesties
> Above the fruited plain.

Walt Whitman, Singer of American Democracy,
expresses this sentiment in his writings. To understand his
theories, we must consider briefly his early environment.
He came from humble farming and sea folk on Long

Island, but spent much of his boyhood about the city of New York. These surroundings secured for the poet a modern, constantly changing civilization and provide his earliest experience with nature.

In addition, he came of good stock. Both his paternal and maternal ancestors had served in Washington's army, so that young Walt had freedom in his blood. From his father he inherited a love of liberty and a sense of simplicity. To his mother may be attributed his interest in religion and the world about him.

The boy Whitman, who later became a genius, lived by the sea, whose mysterious music made him feel in Nature the presence of a friend, a mother, or a god. Many years afterwards, he recalled these pleasant memories in his poems entitled "Sea-Drift" and "The Song of the Bird". As the birds sang, there dawned upon the impressionable boy, the conviction that he too was a singer and a poet. Later in life, he realized that the recalling and the recording of these experiences were greater joys than the experiences themselves.

But his childhood came early to a close. When he reached his eleventh year, he became first an office boy and later a clerk in a lawyer's office, after which he began his journalistic career. At this time he exhibited a tendency to dream – a characteristic which the unthinking failed to realize was constructive, glorified idleness, from which many of his poems were born. Like his Puritan forbears, he did not smoke or drink – his interests were those of God and Nature –not the passing attractions of Man. For the rest of Whitman's life although he worked occasionally with his father as a carpenter, his chief business was writing. Often, while he was at work with his father, he was dreaming, finding material for his next chant.

In his somewhat desultory reading, Whitman came across such notable men as Poe and Bryant, but it was not their works that shaped his future. What made him the man and poet that he became was no following of any hero or master, but his own peculiar genius, that aptitude which enabled him to observe and even love all sorts of conditions and all types of people in the busy life of New York. Indeed, this man now recognized as the father of true American poetry, associated by choice with common crowds, a desire arising from his intense love of, and belief in, democracy of the masses. For instance, he is said to have driven a coach a whole winter for a man who was ill and to have entered eagerly into the lives of the other coach drivers. Part of the material for his famous poem, "I hear America Singing", wherein he describes the songs of the different classes of workmen, was thus obtained. Despite his adaptability and universal interests, however, he was an individualist both in action and in thought.

During the agitation over the slavery issue, Walt Whitman was given a chance to test the permanency of his gospel of democracy and equality, and this opportunity made the man. He went to Washington, where he as poet and Lincoln as commander-in-chief aroused sentiment against slavery. Later he served as a nurse in the Civil War. Since this experience was one of the most influential of his life, naturally it produced noble poetry. Out of these experiences he wrote, "Drum Taps," "My Captain," a glorious tribute to Lincoln, and his beautiful poem, "Vigil strange I kept on the field one night". During the war, he read to the sick who had fallen in battle and was lovingly referred to as the "Man with the face of an angel".

After the war he ventured West. This trip provided a title for one of his poems, "Pioneers". Upon his return he rejoined his father as a carpenter. And as poets have two

great needs, experience and peace, he was quite indifferent to the hurrying thousands of fortune seekers going to the Far West. As time went on, Whitman grew more and more absorbed in his writing, in which he constantly emphasized his love for America and his appreciation of his country's grandeur. Naturally retiring, he said little about his works until his "Leaves of Grass" appeared. Now the peace and the joys of his lonely weeks by the sea were revealed.

At first Whitman's language repelled conventional readers who felt that his poems lacked both rhythm and rhyme, and that his ideas were too radical for his day. He insisted that poetry needed a change, a strong diet of novelty, or it would become feeble. Emerson came across the book and wrote to the then unknown author: "I am not blind to the worth of the wonderful gift of the Leaves of Grass. I find it the most extraordinary piece of wit and wisdom that American has ever contributed. I am very happy in reading it, as great power makes me happy. I give you of your free and brave thought. I have great joy in it. I find incomparable things said incomparably well. I greet you at the beginning of a great career."

The eminent philosopher spoke truly. Today, Whitman's genius is ever in the ascendency. Still another admirer said of him: "Americans abroad may now come home; unto us a man is born."

Yet the creative spirit would permit Whitman no rest. The ever glowing life of New York was around him. His easy gift for making acquaintances helped him to know humanity. As he was fond of music, he met many singers and musicians. Frequently, he visited his friends and told them stories of actual American life and beauty about which he wrote. What was ordinary to many was extraordinary to Whitman. In almost everything, he

found interest and significance, matter for wonder and love. He was seeing poems every day, seeing American beauty in every street, in every face, even in the faces of those from whom men shrank in fear or hatred. Life called for a man like Whitman to discover in a sea of wretchedness, some island on which love could set its foot.

The poet looked upon himself as a preacher of a new religion; he wanted to bring the newest thoughts before the uneducated. The English critic, Symonds, wrote to him: "Who but you is the singer of love and faith in the new advent?" Everything Whitman wrote expressed true Americanism and his belief in a democracy of brother-hood, of passion and charity. He reveled in his love for nature and humanity.

As a singer of American's beauty, Walt Whitman was the spokeman of a whole nation, the prophet and evenage-list of a great idea; a democracy the afforded opportunity to all. His was the healthiest, loftiest, voice of democracy. By imagination and vision, he conveyed the spirit of democracy to the common people. As the voice of Amer-ica singing of men and nature, and inspired by their hopes and ideals, he best portrays the conception of American the Beautiful in these lines: "I hear America singing, the very carols I hear, each singing what belongs to him or her and to none else".

May this thought of a singing world never be lost to American Democracy.

"Mors aut Honorabilis Vita" or "Death or a Life with Honor"

More aut honorabilis vita

Joyce

Joyce Family Crest

CPSIA information can be obtained at www.ICGtesting.com
Printed in the USA
LVOW042341120812

293946LV00004B/2/P